THE CHRISTIAN WORLD

Alan Brown

HODDER
Wayland

an imprint of Hodder Children's Books

Editor
Belinda Hollyer
Picture Research
Caroline Mitchell
Design
Richard Johnson
Production
Rosemary Bishop
Educational consultant
Dr Owen Cole

We are grateful for the advice of the Rev'd
G. B. Mitchell during the preparation of
this book.

We would also like to thank the British
Council of Churches, and the following
members of its Board of Ecumenical Affairs,
for their help as religious advisors:
Mr Martin Conway (Secretary)
Canon Denis Corbishley
Dr Andrew Walker

First published in paperback in Great Britain in 1984
by Macdonald & Co (Publishers) Ltd

This edition published in 2001
by Hodder Wayland, an imprint of
Hodder Children's Books

A catalogue record for this book is available
from the British Library
ISBN 0 7502 3309 5

Printed and bound by Proost in Belgium

Hodder Children's Books
A division of Hodder Headline Ltd
338 Euston Road, London NW1 3BH

Cover picture: A good Friday procession in Jerusalem.
Groups of Christians carry crosses along the route
Jesus is thought to have walked on his way to Calvary,
the hill on which he was crucified.

Endpapers: Bishops from the Greek and Armenian Orthodox
Churches bring new light to the Church of the Holy Sepulchre
on Easter Day. You can read about this ceremony on page 21.

Title page: A procession of young churchgoers in the
Seychelle Islands.

Contents page: Inside the Church of the Holy Sepulchre
in Jerusalem.

Contents

Who are the Christians?

Right: The owner of this market stall has hung a picture of Jesus behind the counter, and decorated it with a garland of flowers. Goa, where the photograph was taken, has a strong Roman Catholic tradition, but it is not only Roman Catholics who use pictures of Jesus in this way. Many Christians hang such pictures to remind themselves of God's presence in everyday life.

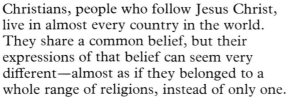

Christians, people who follow Jesus Christ, live in almost every country in the world. They share a common belief, but their expressions of that belief can seem very different—almost as if they belonged to a whole range of religions, instead of only one.

Expressions of faith

There are more than 22,000 Christian groups, and their vivid variety often seems strange, even bewildering. The Zulu churches of southern Africa, the Baptists of North America and the Egyptian Coptic Church have very different traditions, yet all are responding to the same faith. An outdoor service in, say, a Kenyan independent church seems to have little in common with one held in a parish church in England, but both are responding to the same message.

Some Christians expect the leadership of priests; others believe that priests are unnecessary. Some, like the Society of Friends (Quakers), call their gathering place a meeting house rather than a church. Most Christians are baptised, but not, for example, members of the Salvation Army. Roman Catholics have a daily service called the Mass. Other Christians do not share the same beliefs about this service and hold a different one less often—while the Friends and the Salvation Army never celebrate in this way at all!

On a personal level, when Christians pray they may stand, sit, kneel, or lie face down on the floor. They may live apart in a convent and pray for a world they never see, or they may become deeply involved in politics or war. Many people who say they are Christians seldom attend church—and some churches do not seek new members, while others think that is essential.

The centre of faith

The common focus for all these people, and their single unifying force, is Jesus of Nazareth. Each Christian group remembers his life and death, and interprets these in their own way. Christians believe Jesus is the Son of God, who lived on Earth as a human and suffered pain and death, and then rose from the dead. They believe he lives today, and they respond to this with personal faith, and a shared life with others through their churches.

Left: A procession of Christians from a church in Kerala, South India, collecting alms (offerings) for the poor in their district. The cross they carry is a universal Christian symbol. Their use of umbrellas to give the procession a festive touch is shared with some of the ancient Orthodox churches, as you can see from another photograph on page 26.

Far left: Monks are men who have chosen to devote their whole lives to God. Many of them live apart from the rest of the world in communities called monasteries, where they may produce goods to sell to the outside world. This Spanish monk belongs to the Cartujo monastery in Andalusia, which is famous for breeding horses. The church in the background, with its beautiful carved statues, is typical of those built in Europe during the 16th and 17th centuries.

Left: A group of French women wait to join a Holy Week service in their local church. The torch-like candles are a common part of these celebrations; their head scarves are a traditional mark of respect for the holy building in which they are standing.

9

Jesus the Christ

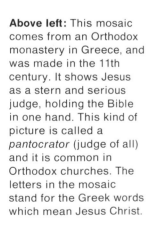

Above left: This mosaic comes from an Orthodox monastery in Greece, and was made in the 11th century. It shows Jesus as a stern and serious judge, holding the Bible in one hand. This kind of picture is called a *pantocrator* (judge of all) and it is common in Orthodox churches. The letters in the mosaic stand for the Greek words which mean Jesus Christ.

Above right: Jesus has emerged from his tomb and stands triumphant over death, holding a banner of victory. The 15th century Italian painter, Piero della Francesca, has clearly shown the marks of the nails on Jesus' hands and feet, and the blood which seeps from a spear wound in his side. It is Jesus' real body that has risen, not a ghost.

Most of the details of Jesus' life are found in the Gospels: four of the books in the Christian Bible. These say that he was born in Bethlehem, in southern Palestine, almost two thousand years ago. He grew up in the town of Nazareth, in a part of northern Palestine called Galilee, with his father Joseph, and his mother Mary.

A new life

When he was about thirty years old Jesus was baptised by a man called John the Baptist, and began a new life of teaching and healing. He travelled through the towns and villages of Palestine with twelve men whom he had chosen to be his companions. This lasted for less than three years (the exact length of time is unknown) until he came into serious conflict with the authorities in Jerusalem, the most important Jewish city in Palestine. Jesus was arrested, tried, condemned to death and then crucified—nailed to a cross until he died.

The Gospels record, however, that within three days Jesus had risen from death. His companions discovered that his tomb was empty, and then reported meeting, talking and sharing meals with him. A few weeks later the companions said they had watched Jesus being taken to heaven by God, promising to return at the end of the world.

The Messiah

John the Baptist, who baptised Jesus, urged people to lead better lives because the Messiah was about to arrive—and Jesus' companions believed that *he* was the Messiah. The word 'Messiah' means 'Anointed One', or 'Christ', and at the time such a person was expected to overthrow Roman rule in Palestine, and restore the Jewish state of Israel to its former greatness.

So the idea of Jesus being the Messiah was dangerous to the Roman authorities, and disturbing to the beliefs of the Jewish leaders.

Jesus did not teach against the Jewish faith. He went to the Temple in Jerusalem, worshipped in synagogues and kept the festivals. He often quoted important Jewish teachings in his sermons and stories. He certainly claimed to forgive sins, however—and since only God could do that, the Jewish leaders believed he was claiming to be divine; something no human ought to do.

A new testament

Jesus was as famous for healing people as for what he said to them. There are many stories in the Gospels about Jesus curing different illnesses, and these acts were taken as a sign that he shared God's power.

Jesus believed he had a special purpose, and he talked about this in sermons and stories. His message was not always straightforward—even his companions found him confusing at times! But one sermon in particular seems to show his ideas of a new way of living:

Happy are the gentle : they shall have the earth as their heritage.
Happy are the merciful : they shall have mercy shown to them.
Happy are the pure in heart : they shall see God.
Happy are those who are persecuted in the cause of right : theirs is the Kingdom of Heaven.

Jesus offered no approval or comfort to the rich and powerful—in fact, he said it was almost impossible for a rich person to enter the kingdom of heaven. He enjoyed the company of people who were disreputable outcasts, and taught that those who were *sure* they were good were the least likely to be accepted by God.

Such deliberate challenges to traditional values were shocking, but his companions and followers clearly believed he was right. The report that Jesus had risen from death —his resurrection—gave them hope. They believed that Jesus had a unique relationship with God, and that because of his resurrection other people could share in his eternal life.

Above left: One Gospel quotes Jesus as saying: "Foxes have holes and the birds of the air have nests, but the Son of Man has nowhere to lay his head." Stanley Spencer, a 20th century British artist, shows Jesus as a human—alone in the desert where he went to pray, without possessions or a home.

Above right: No one knows what Jesus, a Palestinian Jew, looked like—and so Christians from different lands show him in the ways which make sense to them. In this Chinese painting Jesus is talking to Mary Magdalene, one of his followers. The halo of gold light which surrounds Jesus' head is a western artistic tradition, but the rest of the picture is entirely Chinese.

The good news spreads

Pentecost

After Jesus had risen from the dead and had been taken to heaven, his companions gathered together for the Jewish festival of Pentecost. The book in the Bible called the Acts of the Apostles says that they suddenly heard "a powerful wind from heaven, the noise of which filled the entire house in which they were sitting; and something appeared to them that seemed like tongues of fire; these separated and came to rest on the head of each of them. They were all filled with the Holy Spirit, and began to speak in foreign languages as the Spirit gave them the gift of speech"

This experience gave the companions courage and faith to go out into the world, teaching and preaching what they had learned from Jesus' life, death and resurrection. The companions had been called the disciples of Jesus; now they were called the apostles—from a Greek word which means 'sent as messengers'. The apostles believed they were sent to spread the good news of the risen Christ.

Saint Peter

One of the companions, Simon, had been given a new name by Jesus: Peter, which means 'rock' in Greek. He is usually thought to have been the companions' leader but very little is known about his life, except that he had been a fisherman until he joined Jesus. Peter was also married; his mother-in-law is mentioned in one of the Gospels.

Christian writings show Peter as a determined leader, who realised that Jesus' message should not be kept only for the Jews. There is a strong tradition that he travelled to Rome, and became that city's first bishop. It is also believed that he too was crucified: in Rome, during the Emperor Nero's persecution of Christians.

Other traditions

Even less is known about the other apostles. One, called John, probably travelled to Ephesus in modern Turkey; another named Thomas may have gone to India and founded a Christian community there. Many villages and cities claim to have been visited by one of the apostles, but there is no certainty about any of these—all that is clear is that the new Christian message spread rapidly.

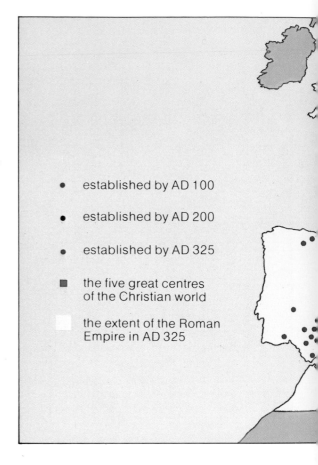

- • established by AD 100
- • established by AD 200
- • established by AD 325
- ■ the five great centres of the Christian world
- ☐ the extent of the Roman Empire in AD 325

Saint Paul

Paul was a great figure among the early Christians. His Hebrew name was Saul, and he was involved in some of the persecutions of Jesus' followers which followed Jesus' death. But while he was travelling to Damascus to root out Jesus' followers in that city, Saul had a vision of Jesus that changed his life. Filled with a new faith in the Christ Jesus, he spent several years in quiet thought before beginning to preach. Then, taking the Greek name of Paul, he became a powerful Christian teacher.

More is known about Paul than any other apostle because some of his letters have survived. These show him to be a well-educated man with strong views, full of energy, and passionately committed to taking the message of the risen Christ to gentiles—people who were not Jewish.

Paul travelled widely around the Mediterranean on three great journeys, visiting churches and establishing new ones. His letters were mostly written to such new groups of Christians, and contain advice, encouragement and correction. Paul died in Rome, perhaps at the same time as Peter.

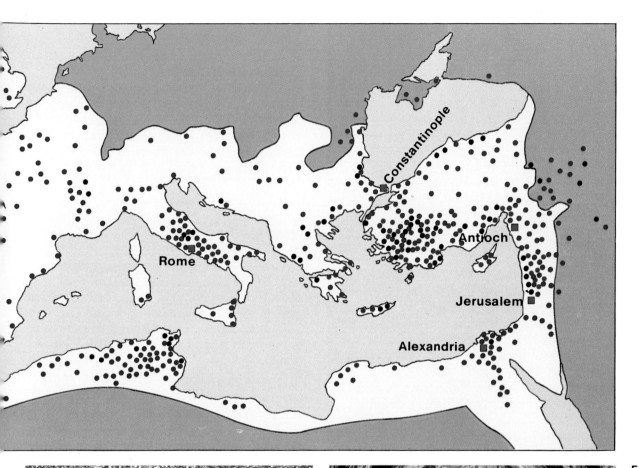

Far left: This mosaic of Saint Paul comes from a 5th century Italian church. He carries two of his letters, and the Roman robes he wears are the sort from which Christian priests' robes were later developed. No one knows if this 2nd century description of Paul is an accurate one: "small in size, with meeting eyebrows and a rather large nose, bald-headed and strongly built".

Left: Matthew's Gospel records that Jesus said to Peter: "I will give you the keys of the Kingdom of Heaven." So Peter is usually shown holding at least one key, as in this 13th century altar painting from London's Westminster Abbey.

The early church

The word 'church' can have a number of meanings. It can refer to all Christians throughout the world; or it can refer to individual groups like the Orthodox Church or the Baptist Church; or it can refer to the building in which worship takes place. During the first three hundred years of the Christian church there were no special buildings, no separately organised groups, and Christianity had not become an established religion. But by the end of the fourth century after Jesus' death much had happened that was to shape today's faith.

Gentiles as well as Jews

Jesus' first followers were Jews, but many gentiles (non-Jews) were also attracted by the apostles' teachings. Did they have to become Jews in order to become Christians?

There were two main issues—the Jewish custom of circumcision for all males, and the Jewish food laws. Both Peter and Paul, but especially Paul, argued that gentile Christians had equal rights with Jewish Christians, and did not have to become Jews first. In one of his letters Paul says that Christians had no distinctions "between Jew and Greek, slave and free, male and female, but all of you are one in Christ Jesus".

Church authority

As the apostles died, others took their place as leaders. Usually each separate group chose a bishop—preferably someone who had known one of the apostles and could continue their work. Then, as the groups multiplied and grew, bishops became responsible for the care of people within a larger area: the bishops of Rome, Jerusalem, Constantinople, Alexandria and Antioch became the most influential of these.

Although other forms of church government existed the bishops were the most important, and they claimed the authority of the first apostles. This question of authority, of who should decide on religious matters, was to play a crucial role in later differences within the Christian family.

Early worship

At first, Christians continued to visit synagogues and to practise Jewish customs. But later they began to gather for worship on the first day of the week instead of on the Jewish Sabbath, the last day of the week. This grew from their belief that Jesus rose from death on that day, and it marked a stage in their move away from Jewish origins towards a universal faith. Easter and Pentecost were important festivals, but Christmas does not seem to have been celebrated at all. Jesus' resurrection was considered more important than his birth.

Clearly, many people were attracted by Christian teaching. Less than one hundred years after Jesus died the Roman historian Pliny wrote that Christians worshipped in the countryside as well as the towns of the Roman Empire: "It is their habit, on a fixed day, to assemble before daylight and to recite by turns a form of words to Christ as God." Another historian considered the Christians to be a dangerous group of people, "given to a new and wicked superstition", and they were sometimes persecuted, often in very harsh ways. This ended, however, with the Roman Emperor Constantine, who became a Christian himself in AD 312. By the end of the fourth century, Christianity was the official religion throughout the Roman Empire.

Right: Early Christian symbols. The monogram (top left) is the Chi–Rho. Chi (X) and Rho (P) are the first two letters of 'Christ' in the Greek alphabet.

An anchor was used to show hope and certainty. The fish curved around it represents Christ, and beside it is 'fish' in Greek. Each letter in that word also stands for the initial letters in the Greek phrase 'Jesus Christ God's Son Saviour'.

Alpha and Omega (below right) are the first and last letters in the Greek alphabet. The Christian Bible says that God is "Alpha and Omega, the beginning and end".

The dove with an olive branch is an ancient symbol of peace. Christians used it to show their belief that Jesus offers the hope of everlasting peace.

Left and below: These pictures come from the catacombs in Rome, where some early groups of Christians met for secret worship. The paintings on the walls of the narrow underground passages are among the first examples of Christian art.

The painting on the left shows Jesus as a 'good shepherd', caring for a flock of sheep while he scatters seeds for future harvest. Images like this were very common in the religious art of the time. Jesus is shown in the same way as other gods and kings.

The painting below is more obviously Christian. Jesus is shown with some of his companions, in a scene which could be related to many of the New Testament stories.

The Christian Bible

The Christian Bible contains the complete Jewish Bible, called the Old Testament by Christians. To this was added a collection of books written during the hundred or so years after Jesus, which is known as the New Testament.

The Epistles
The earliest known Christian writings are Paul's letters, often called 'epistles'—the Greek word for 'letters'. He pays little attention to Jesus' life, and concentrates instead on what that life, death and resurrection mean to Christians. Paul's letters were probably written before the first Gospel. The New Testament also contains other letters, which were thought to have been written by Peter, John and some of the other apostles.

The Gospels
The word 'gospel' means 'good news', and the four Gospels in the New Testament provide the only available record of Jesus' life. None was written by Jesus; they were compiled between thirty and seventy years after his death. Little is known for certain about the Gospel writers, although some traditions associate the Gospels of Matthew and John with Jesus' disciples of the same names.

The final collection
The Christian Bible took centuries to reach its present form. The collection was finally agreed at a council in Carthage in AD 397. Even now, though, there is not complete agreement, for the Roman Catholic Church includes a group of Jewish writings called the Apocrypha, as well as the Old and New Testaments. Other churches do not usually accept the Apocrypha.

The Bible's place
The Bible readings which take place in churches remind the faithful of Jesus' life and teachings. In most churches the Bible reading forms the basis of the minister's sermon, or talk. Many churches follow a set pattern of readings, so that almost all the Old and New Testaments can be read out during the year.

Interpretation
Christians have had many arguments about how the Bible should be used. Some say it is the real, unchanging word of God, and must be taken literally: it cannot be argued with, or altered in any way. Others think that it was written by the people of a particular time, who were certainly inspired by God, but who were also influenced by their own ideas. This means that what they wrote can be questioned, compared, and freely discussed.

But all Christians agree that they should study the Bible. It provides knowledge about Jesus and his understanding of God, and it is the basis and the chief source of the churches' teachings.

Natiuitas xpi in bethleem iudæ magi munera offerunt
et infantes occiduntur

Central beliefs

Far right: The Trinity has been pictured in many different ways, but this 15th century stained glass window from Germany shows the most common idea. God the Father, the largest figure, holds the cross on which God the Son, Jesus, is crucified. Between them hovers the Holy Spirit, shown as a dove.

Below: The Last Judgement. Christian tradition says that Jesus will return at the end of the world, to judge the living and the dead. This 15th century Italian painting shows people emerging from their graves to meet God. Jesus is surrounded by saints and angels, with the Virgin Mary (his mother) on his right. Devils claim the damned for hell, while angels lead the fortunate into the garden of heaven.

Few Christians today think heaven and hell are actual places. While some believe only the faithful will be saved, others are sure that, in the end, God will include everyone in the kingdom of heaven.

Christians believe that Jesus was the Christ and the Son of God. Jesus died for the sake of all people, as the Old Testament had promised; he was buried but rose from death, also as the Old Testament had promised. And his triumph over death was witnessed by his companions. These events are central to the Christian faith.

Christians do not claim to have all the answers, yet they believe that Jesus revealed God's purpose in a new way, as a human. But it is because they believe he was also raised from the dead and is alive now, in them, with God and for all time, that they choose to commit themselves to him.

The Trinity

Perhaps the most mysterious of all Christian beliefs is the Trinity. God, it is believed, is one God: there has always been only one, and since God cannot change, there will always be only one. But Christians also refer to God in three ways—as God the Father and creator; as the God the Son, Jesus Christ; and as God the Holy Spirit, the power of God which people experience in their lives.

Christians find this way of describing God helps them to refer to the wide range of their experience, but it is important to remember that the words just try to capture that experience. Christians also believe that God cannot be limited by words, or completely understood by humans.

The Incarnation

Almost all Christians believe that Jesus was both God and also human. God the Son became human in Jesus, and so Jesus was both these things. Traditional Christianity has always argued that Jesus was fully human and fully divine.

Through this incarnation—his becoming flesh and blood—God gave people a way to reach him.

Sin and Atonement

Sin is what separates people from God. When people sin, Christians believe, they misuse the freedom God has given them. Instead of responding to his love, people follow their own desires—and so their actions take them further away from God. It is as if the 'real' relationship between God and humans is blurred by human faults.

Jesus' death and resurrection is seen as the way in which people can find the true relationship with God. One method of explaining this is to say that Jesus paid for human mistakes through his own death. When he died, he destroyed the effects of sins. Christians call this atonement ('at-one-ment'): the bringing together of God and people.

The Creeds

Many of the central beliefs are expressed in the creeds (statements of belief), particularly the Apostles' Creed and the

Nicene Creed. In many churches today one of these is said during services. Creeds were first used during baptism ceremonies, as a clear statement of faith. Later they were written as safeguards against wrong ideas. The Apostles' Creed says:

I believe in God, the Father almighty, creator of heaven and earth. I believe in Jesus Christ, his only Son, our Lord. He was conceived by the power of the Holy Spirit and born of the Virgin Mary. He suffered under Pontius Pilate, was crucified, died and was buried. He descended to the dead. On the third day he rose again. He ascended into heaven, and is seated at the right hand of the Father. He will come again to judge the living and the dead. I believe in the Holy Spirit, the holy catholic Church, the communion of saints, the forgiveness of sins, the resurrection of the body, and the life everlasting. Amen.

Faith

Christians vary about some of these beliefs, but the centre for every Christian is faith in Jesus Christ. Many ordinary members of the church have only a hazy idea about the exact detail of the teachings, but they rely upon a strong faith to help them towards an understanding.

The faith that Christians hope to have is the sort Jesus showed: that God is loving and faithful, and his goodness will finally triumph over evil and death.

The Orthodox Churches

The word 'orthodox' means true or right worship, and Orthodox Churches trace their history back to the beginnings of Christianity. The map on page 10 shows the five great centres of the early church, from which separate eastern and western traditions developed. The four eastern churches and Rome separated in 1054, and the eastern churches continued to share ideas among themselves. They became the established religion in countries such as Russia, Greece and Armenia. They do not recognise the absolute power of any one leader; authority usually lies with a group of bishops. Each Orthodox Church has its own language and customs, but they all share a living tradition of worship.

An Orthodox service

All the senses are used during an Orthodox service. The smell and smoke of incense drifts through the air, the priest chants the words of the service and is answered in song by the choir and the congregation. Icons (holy pictures) are often richly decorated with gold paint and surrounded by flickering candles, and the worshippers move around to pray before these, bowing and kissing them as a sign of love and respect. The whole building—often lit only by candles—is filled with mystery and drama, represented in many different ways.

The architecture of religion

An Orthodox church is designed to represent the universe. The ceiling stands for heaven, so it is there that large icons of Jesus usually appear. The floor of the church represents the world, and most Orthodox churches do not have seats for the worshippers: they stand, and move about, during services.

At the far end of the church from the entrance is the sanctuary, where the altar, or holy table, stands. The sanctuary is separated from the 'world' of the main part of the church by a huge screen. This is called an iconostasis, and the icons which cover it show pictures of Jesus' life, and of the Gospel writers. Worshippers can only glimpse the altar, hidden behind the screen —just as they cannot clearly see God, which it represents. Only the priests, on behalf of the people, may open the screen's doors and enter this part of the church.

Right: A Greek Orthodox congregation gathers around the priest during the Divine Liturgy, to hear the Gospel reading. You can see icons on the wall in the background, which are reflecting candlelight from the centre of the church. These pictures are of saints, angels and famous religious figures.

The Divine Liturgy

Every Sunday, and on other special festival days, Orthodox churches celebrate their most important service: the Divine Liturgy. It is seen as a re-enactment of the birth, life, death and resurrection of Jesus. During this service the priest carries bread and wine to the altar behind the screen. When he returns, it is believed, the bread and wine he carries have been transformed by the Holy Spirit into the body and blood of Jesus. In this way the people share Jesus' sacrifice.

An Orthodox Easter

There is a picture of an Orthodox Easter ceremony inside the covers of this book. The worshippers have been waiting for hours, in the darkened church, for Easter Sunday: the day which marks Jesus' rising from death. At midnight a new light is created on the altar, and carried out into the church. From that first light other candles are lit, until everyone holds part of what they believe Jesus represents: the 'light of the world'. Then bells peal out, and the celebration of Easter begins with processions, singing, and services of thanksgiving.

Left: During the Liturgy bread is blessed by the priest, and shared out among people after the service. This is a different ceremony from the bread and wine offered during the service, and it is called an *agape*, or love feast. It is a symbol of the shared love among Christians.

In this picture a Greek Orthodox priest is distributing the *agape* bread outside the church. Anyone can share in this offering.

Left: Many Christians offer music to God; the Ethiopian Church offers dance as well. This picture shows the dance of the Debteras (elders) on Saint Michael's Day in Addis Ababa. It is performed outside the Church of Saint Michael, and is a slow and stately dance of graceful beauty.

The Roman Catholic Church

Above: The custom of lighting candles as a part of prayer is common in Roman Catholic churches. They are called votive (offering) candles, and are usually placed in stands near a holy statue or picture. Worshippers buy and light a candle, and stand for a few minutes in silent prayer. The candle is a visible sign of their contact with God.

Roman Catholics trace their history back to Peter, the apostle whom Jesus called 'the rock'. They believe that when his missionary travels were over Peter settled in Rome, and became their church's leader and bishop. The Pope, who heads the Roman Catholic Church, is still called the Bishop of Rome. His leadership is seen as descending directly from Peter, and so in turn from Jesus himself. This gives him a unique position in the Christian church, for no other leader claims such complete authority. The word 'catholic' means 'universal', and shows that it is a world-wide organisation. Its headquarters are in Rome, in an independent state called the Vatican City.

A sacramental church

More than half of the world's Christians are Roman Catholics. To be a member of this church is to share a faith with about eight hundred million other people. In life and death, in sickness and health, and through the most important events of people's lives, the church provides help, guidance, and a firm structure of religious meaning. A sacrament is a visible sign of God's power,

and the Roman Catholic Church has seven sacraments which mark the most important ways people can receive that power.

The first is baptism. All babies are baptised soon after birth, which brings them into the care of the whole church family. When they are about seven, children receive their First Communion. They receive the bread which, it is believed, has become the body of Christ. Now they can share fully in the great sacrament of the Mass, the central act of worship and thanksgiving for all Roman Catholics. Another sacrament called Confirmation occurs when children are about twelve, and ready to make their own commitment.

The other sacraments are marriage; confession (where people can restore their relationship with God by showing they are sorry for their sins); and unction, or healing, used with the sick and dying. The seventh sacrament is ordination, when trained men are made priests by their local bishop.

A faith for life

The church, the family and education form a triangle of experience on which Roman Catholics can build. Regular worship, learning about the faith, and understanding the relationship between God and the world are all very important.

On some matters the church's teachings are firm. The promises of marriage, for example, are made in front of God—and so divorce cannot be recognised. Artificial birth control is also forbidden, for the church teaches that no human should interfere with the creation of life, a gift from God.

The changing church

Since 1965, the year in which a general council of bishops recommended many changes, aspects of Roman Catholicism have changed. The Mass is no longer conducted in Latin, but in each country's local language. Many nuns and priests no longer wear traditional clothes, and have become closely involved in the ordinary world.

Where millions of people and thousands of priests are concerned, there will always be differences of opinion. But the Roman Catholic Church manages to contain its debates within itself—and to offer comfort, security and authority to the vast number of Christians who are its members.

Left: A young South American girl prepares to enter church for her First Communion, helped by a nun. The girl wears white as a symbol of purity. Her white prayerbook and rosary beads are probably presents from family or friends, to mark the importance of the occasion.

Below: The altar is the focus of attention in all Roman Catholic churches, and here in a side chapel in Chartres Cathedral it is decorated with candles and flowers, as a sign of devotion. The statue of the Virgin Mary behind the altar is also richly decorated, and you can see the baby Jesus in her arms. There are stands for votive candles on either side of the sanctuary (the area which contains the altar).

The Protestant Churches

Above: The Lutheran pastor of a Swedish church stands in the pulpit to give his sermon. It is an evening service; at other times the church would be brightly lit. The pastor is wearing a cassock, a tradition which is shared by many other Christian ministers.

There are thousands of different Protestant churches, and all of them grew out of *protest*: about the Christian church in general, or about one part of it in particular. Protestant origins go back further than the 16th century, but it was then that men like Martin Luther and John Calvin condemned false teaching in the Roman Catholic church, and provided a new way for Christians to express their beliefs.

Luther and Calvin
The Lutheran churches of Europe and North America trace their origins to Martin Luther, a Roman Catholic monk who protested about the ways in which his church abused its power. (In his day, for example, it was widely believed that people could buy special merit from the church, and so ensure themselves a place in heaven.) Luther taught that people are accepted by God through their own faith, rather than by following all the church's teachings.

John Calvin, too, believed that faith, rather than doing good things, was central. He rejected the authority of the Roman Catholic Church and its priests, and most of its festivals and ceremonies. He also rejected the importance of the Virgin Mary, Jesus' mother—none of this, he said, related to the Bible's teachings. Calvin's teachings were especially important to the development of the Presbyterian Church.

The Protestant tradition
Protestant churches are generally plain and simple buildings. They do not often contain statues or pictures, incense is not used, and saints' days are not celebrated.

The centre of a Protestant service is the Bible. A pulpit is usually in an important position, and it is from this stand that the minister preaches a sermon, based on the Bible's teaching. In some United Reformed churches the services begin by carrying in the Bible, which is placed open on the pulpit or a table. At the end of the service the Bible is closed, and carried out again before the people leave. Through the preaching and the Bible, Protestants believe, they have direct access to God. There is no need for a priest to represent them—they have a personal responsibility for their own belief.

Prayer and singing, too, play an important part in worship. Prayers are often made up by a minister, rather than read from a book.

The Anglican Communion
The Church of England is also called the Anglican, or Episcopalian, Church. It began in England but branches of it are found all over the world, and they are all part of what is referred to as the Anglican Communion.

The Anglican church is not simply a Protestant one. Many of its churches are plain and simple, but others look just like Roman Catholic ones, with candles, statues, incense, and chapels in honour of the Virgin Mary. These contrasts show how Anglicans try to balance reform with Catholic traditions.

This attitude does not suit everyone, however, and breakaway groups have gained many members over the years. The Congregationalists believe that each congregation is responsible for its own affairs, rather than a bishop. Methodism sprang from the teachings of John Wesley in the 18th century. It was originally an Anglican revival movement, and used the same prayer book, but Methodists now have a separate, world-wide church.

Individual faith
Some Protestant churches have bishops as leaders; others use councils of ministers. Most have the sacraments of baptism and Communion. All Protestants, however, insist that the Bible is the heart of their teaching, and that individual Christians are responsible for their own life and faith.

Left: The congregation of a Baptist church in Britain singing a hymn. You can see copies of the Bible resting in front of them, for use in another part of the service.

Below: An Anglican priest in South Africa, talking to some members of his church's congregation. Anglican priests are sometimes called vicars, which means deputies, or representatives. A vicar's duties include visiting homes and representing the church at local meetings and councils, as well as holding church services.

The Pentecostal Movement

The Christian festival of Pentecost marks the occasion when the apostles experienced the Holy Spirit's powerful presence, promised to them by Jesus. They also received the gift of speaking in foreign languages – often translated as 'speaking in tongues'. This double gift has been at the heart of the modern Pentecostal movement. There are more than 200 Pentecostal churches in the United States, and hundreds more throughout the world. They are probably the fastest-growing Christian movement.

It began in the United States, partly in response to very formal church worship, and partly, Pentecostalists believe, through the actions of the Holy Spirit. Worshippers experience the Holy Spirit's presence in a direct and personal way. They believe in prophecy (the foretelling of events) and religious visions, and in the ability to speak 'in tongues'. Such speech can sometimes be identified as a foreign language, but speaking in unknown languages – a collection of spontaneous sounds – is also common. Pentecostalists regard this as a way of expressing their close relationship with God.

The Pentecostal tradition

In the early years of the twentieth century Pentecostal groups in the United States drew their support from such people as black and poor white Americans, who had often been rejected by other churches. They formed groups with names like the Apostolic Faith Movement, the Assembly of God, and the Pentecostal Holiness Church, exploring new ways to express faith together.

Most Pentecostalists enjoy informal acts of worship, and use powerful preaching and rhythmic singing and chanting. The role of healing is stressed, and ministers often claim that God can heal people through the Holy Spirit. This is sometimes seen as a way of dealing with sin – for sin can lead to physical or mental illness, and to cure such things is to release people from the evil power of the devil.

A modern influence

Recent interest by many Christians in spontaneous acts of worship has led to a renewal of Pentecostal ideas – but this time, most believers have remained within their own churches. This means that Pentecostal, or charismatic, Christians are represented within the Roman Catholic and Protestant churches. (The word 'charismatic' means 'gift', and such Christians put their faith in the Holy Spirit's traditional gifts of love, joy and peace.)

Right: A Pentecostal service in the United States of America. Some heads are bowed in silent prayer, but other members of the group have felt the presence of the Holy Spirit urging them to call out expressions of faith and love. Each person is free to offer their own prayers to the whole group.

The meeting is an unusually small one. This large modern church is generally packed with members, and special classes are also held for young children.

Left: These Pentecostal Christians have made a pilgrimage (religious journey) from the United States to the holy city of Jerusalem. Here they are gathered for a meeting of prayer and song, and the preacher lifts his hands in encouragement to the large crowd. He will lead their hymn singing and their statements of faith. He may be able to offer the gift of healing to sick people—and he will certainly urge his listeners to seek the power of the Holy Spirit in their lives. Nearly all Pentecostalists believe that Jesus Christ will return to this world: literally, and in the near future.

Family differences

Right: Some of the ancient traditions of the Ethiopian Church are not shared by other Christian groups. This picture shows the procession of the Holy Arks of the Covenant, in Addis Ababa. The Arks are stone tablets, on which the Gospels have been inscribed. These are a link with the history of Christianity, for in ancient times the Jewish religion had an Ark of the Covenant, on which the Ten Commandments were inscribed.

Each year, on the eve of the festival of Epiphany, the Ethiopian Arks are carried through the streets of Addis Ababa to a nearby field. Church members spend the night there in prayer, before the next day's celebrations begin.

If a Christian were to move from the Russian Orthodox Church to the Southern Baptist Church of the United States, a remarkable change in worship would be part of the experience. The buildings not only look different; they serve very different roles for their congregations, and so they are thought of in entirely separate ways. The same would be true of the words used in services, the place of the church leaders, and so forth. Yet both churches trace their origins and practices to the same Gospels, and both respond to the same person: Jesus Christ.

Every church has its own particular history, style and outlook, shaped in part by the surrounding society. Many recognise the rights of other groups to call themselves Christians, and acknowledge a shared heritage with them. Other groups believe that only their way of worship represents true belief, and so think that any deviation from their customs is dangerously wrong. Today such opinions are often expressed in less rigid ways than in the past, but the heritage of misunderstanding and mistrust—even hatred—can still be a strong one, especially between Catholic and Protestant.

Right: Elizabeth Canham is an Anglican priest. Although she is English, she had to be ordained in the United States because the Church of England did not allow women to become priests until the early 1990s. Today women can become priests in most provinces of the Anglican Church. However, only Brazil, Central America, Mexico, Canada, the USA, Ireland, Southern Africa, New Zealand and Japan allow women priests to become bishops.

A history of differences

Such differences may seem strange, but there is a long tradition of debate, disagreement and dispute within the Christian family. This was first recorded between Peter and Paul, whose disagreements about the observance of the Jewish food laws for early Christians are stated in the Bible. In one sense, perhaps, the church's history can be seen as one of strong individuals and movements, whose arguments have helped to shape a lively and vigorous faith.

The ordination of women

Perhaps the most important dispute for many Christians today concerns the ordination of women as priests and ministers of the church. Many women believe that Jesus has called them to his ministry, and a number of churches have responded to that belief by revising the rules which have prevented their ordination. Methodists, for example, ordain women as ministers, while some parts of the Anglican church have women priests and others do not. The Roman Catholic church resists the change entirely, despite growing pressure, while the Orthodox churches have not yet considered the issue important. This may be a major difference among Christians for many years to come.

Politics and faith

There have often been heated arguments about the political role of Christianity, and this century is no exception. Many Christians feel that faith and politics are entirely separate matters, while others believe that Jesus' message demands their involvement—in changing the world's inequalities, or supporting a particular political party, or protesting against war or modern weapons like the atomic bomb.

Diversity, not division

Christian groups care deeply about their traditions, their understanding of Jesus, their way of expressing truth in worship, and their chosen pattern of obedience to God. Most Christians accept this reflection of human individuality, and value the rich diversity such differences offer. The divisions which arise from quarrels and hatred are another matter, however, and cannot easily be justified or accepted.

Left: The Salvation Army was founded in the 19th century, to take the Gospel message to the poor and needy in the new industrial cities. Its members wear a uniform and follow a strict code of behaviour, but the style of their teaching is lively and spirited. The tambourines and banners in the picture are typical Army traditions.

Unlike most Christian groups, the Salvation Army does not celebrate the Communion service at all. It believes that the service encourages divisions among Christians, because they do not all share it in the same way.

Servants in authority

The Gospel of John records Jesus washing his companions' feet. The Gospel tells of Peter's protest at this—and of Jesus' reply.

"You call me Master and Lord," said Jesus, "and rightly; so I am. If I, then, the Lord and Master, have washed your feet, you should wash each other's feet. I have given you an example so that you may copy what I have done for you."

In this act of service Jesus set an example for all Christian leaders. It is a reminder to them that they are there to serve others, and to minister to them. That is why some churches use the word 'minister' of their leader, and why Baptists and the Christian Brethren use the word 'pastor'—a Latin term which means 'shepherd'. The word 'priest' is used by the Roman Catholic, Orthodox and Anglican churches.

Training to serve
Whatever their title, priests, pastors and ministers usually train before they can begin their work. The length of time for this varies, but it may be more than four years before fulltime service can begin. Roman Catholic, Orthodox and Anglican priests are ordained when their training is completed. During this ceremony a bishop lays his hands on their heads, as a sign of God's help.

Some churches have another group of ministers, called deacons. Deacons also train, and do much the same work as priests and ministers, but they do not take the Communion service.

The senior servants
A bishop is a senior priest or minister, who is given responsibility for the people of a whole area, rather than a single church. An archbishop has greater responsibility still—sometimes for the whole of the church in one country.

In the Orthodox churches the senior archbishops are called patriarchs, which means 'great fathers'. In the Roman Catholic Church a special importance is given to a group of men called cardinals. The cardinals elect the Pope, who serves as the supreme head of their church.

In England, Anglican bishops and archbishops are appointed by the Queen, who is the head of the Church of England. In other countries, such as Australia, New

Zealand, Hong Kong and Canada they are elected. Many Protestant churches elect their national leaders (moderator, president, and so on) each year. These people rule their groups through councils of ministers and elders, who are elected by individual churches.

The agent of God
The Orthodox and Roman Catholic churches believe that priests represent the people, and are the agents through whom the church members reach out to God, and through whom God responds. The central services of these churches, the Divine Liturgy and the Mass, use a priest to offer bread and wine to God on the people's behalf. It is through the priest that the bread and wine become the body and blood of Jesus Christ.

Ministers and leaders
Protestant churches believe that their minister is simply the person who leads the church members. For them, God speaks through the Bible and the Holy Spirit rather than a priest, but they care deeply about the quality of the minister's preaching.

Left: The Patriarch of the Armenian Orthodox Church is their most important leader. Here he is shown washing the feet of one of his fellow priests during a Holy Week service. This ceremony reminds everyone of the occasion when Jesus washed the feet of his companions. In the foreground is the butter which will be blessed later in the service, and used to make the sign of the cross.

Below: The African Israel Nineveh Church is the largest independent church in Kenya. Here, two of its ministers are preaching the Bible's message at an outdoor meeting. Preaching is one of the most important tasks of a church leader, for it is a way of telling people about God's purposes for the world.

Places of worship

Right: The Cathedral of Christ and Our Lady in Durham is one of the most famous cathedrals in Great Britain, and its history dates back to the beginning of the 11th century. The foundation stones for the present building were laid in 1093, and the building was completed in 1128. The Galilee Chapel, at the western end, was added in 1175. It contains the tomb of the Venerable Bede, an early English saint.

Durham Cathedral was once the headquarters of a Benedictine monastery. The monastery buildings still exist, although we have not included them in the picture.

There is a small 12th-century church in a village called Taizé, in France. Enter it on a bright summer's day and you enter absolute blackness. The contrast between light and dark is shocking. If you feel your way to a seat and sit down, your eyes slowly become accustomed to the dark. You begin to notice other figures sitting around you. They, too, are sitting in silence in the dark, cool church. This place of worship encourages silence. It helps the worshippers to think, and sets them apart from the glaring light of day.

Christians can worship anywhere, but they have built churches since the end of the 3rd century. Each different design—and there are many—is meant to help them find a way to express their faith. The darkness of the old church in Taizé contrasts with the bright airy lightness of a Lutheran church in Germany or Finland, and with the splendidly rich decorations of other groups.

Church features

The earliest churches were usually rectangular, with a semi-circular niche in one of the shorter sides: the drawing on the left shows this sort of layout. The leaders sat around the edge of the semi-circle, and the rest of the church members sat in the main part of the building. The altar was placed in front of the niche, between the leaders and the rest of the members.

In today's Roman Catholic or Anglican church the altar, or holy table, is the focus of attention. It used always to stand at the eastern end of the building but this is no longer true—sometimes it stands in the very centre of the church.

In an Orthodox church the altar cannot be seen, for it is concealed behind a great screen covered with holy pictures. And some Protestant churches do not have an altar at all. The centre of attention is the pulpit, from which the minister talks to the people, and there is a table for Communion services. Each of these differences tells you something about the beliefs of the Christians who worship there.

When there is an altar or pulpit, church members will sit facing it, or form a circle around it, or look down on it from an upstairs gallery. But the Friends do not use either an altar or a pulpit, and so they face each other in a circle or square. Their places

Above: This building style is called a basilica. It was adapted from a Roman design.

Galilee Chapel

font

of worship are called meeting houses, and some Protestants use the word 'chapel' instead of 'church'.

Cathedrals

Cathedrals are usually just extremely large churches. A cathedral is the church which contains the local bishop's seat, or throne; it can be thought of as the bishop's headquarters. Many cathedrals are famous for their music, and often have choir schools attached to them where young children are trained in singing as part of their education.

Variety and difference

Find out for yourself, next time you visit a town or city, how many churches, chapels and other Christian places of worship there are. There will probably be many—and their differences will be surprising!

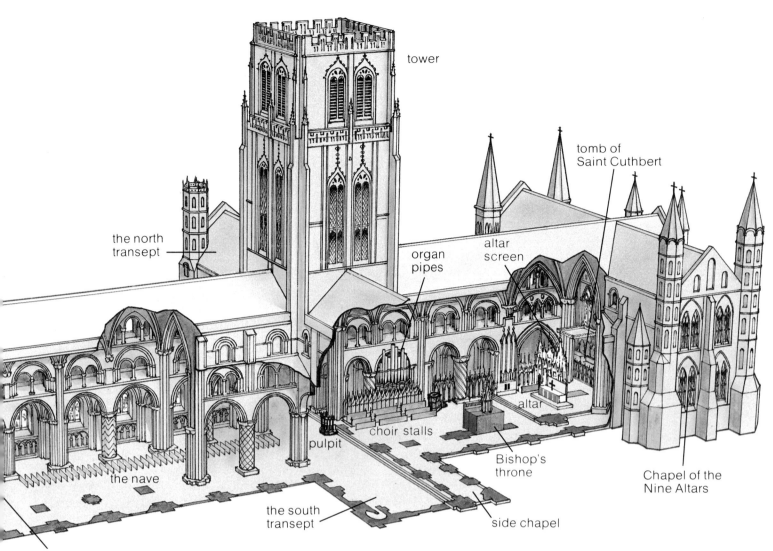

tower

the north
transept

organ
pipes

altar
screen

tomb of
Saint Cuthbert

altar

choir stalls

pulpit

Bishop's
throne

the nave

the south
transept

side chapel

Chapel of the
Nine Altars

main door

Left: Christian worship
does not have to take
place inside a building.
This South African church
holds its services in the
open air, and all the
necessary equipment is
taken from village to
village, and set up on the
spot.

Personal prayer

Our Father in heaven, hallowed be your name, your kingdom come, your will be done, on earth as in heaven. Give us today our daily bread. Forgive us our sins as we forgive those who sin against us. Lead us not into temptation, but deliver us from evil. For the kingdom, the power and the glory are yours, now and for ever. Amen.

This prayer is based on the one Jesus taught his companions, to show how people should pray. It is called the Lord's Prayer, and is frequently used in every church.

There are times for private prayer in most church services, as well as moments when everyone prays together. But Christians are also encouraged to make time in their everyday lives to pray alone. They believe that God knows their needs before they pray, but prayer helps them to develop a personal relationship with him.

Types of prayer

All Christians use prayer to thank God for his blessings, and to acknowledge his love and care for the world. Many ask God to help particular people during difficult times.

This is called intercession; a way of linking the person who prays both with God, and with those who are being prayed for.

God is also asked to forgive people. Christians know that, despite their efforts, they fail to do God's will. Their mistakes mean that they are not worthy of God's love. But they believe that if they ask God to forgive them he will do so, if they truly try to change their ways.

Methods of prayer

Most Christians do not have set times for prayer, though many say a prayer of thanks before meals. Others pray at night, or at various times in the day. Some use a set form of words; others pray spontaneously.

There is no one position for prayer, but it is common for Christians to kneel, and to press their hands together in front of them. Some make the sign of the cross in front of their bodies, to remind themselves of the way in which Jesus died.

Christians often use a holy picture or statue, or a cross or crucifix, to help them concentrate and feel close to God. Many others think about a passage from the Bible.

Right: Rosaries are used as an aid to prayer by many Christians, especially Roman Catholics. This picture shows how the Catholic rosary is used.

The prayers begin at the crucifix, which hangs from the string of beads. When the main circle of beads is reached, the prayers are grouped into five parts.

Before each group of prayers is said, the worshipper thinks about certain events in Jesus' life. These are chosen from the Joyful Mysteries (such as his birth); the Sorrowful Mysteries (such as his death); or the Glorious Mysteries (such as his resurrection).

There are five Mysteries in each of these groups of events, to match the five sections of small beads. Only one group of Mysteries is usually considered at any time.

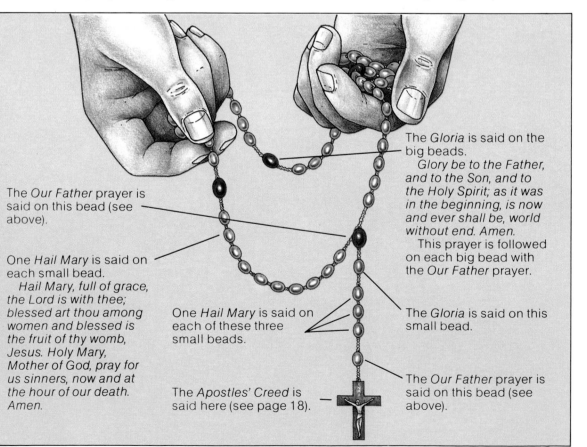

The *Our Father* prayer is said on this bead (see above).

One *Hail Mary* is said on each small bead.
Hail Mary, full of grace, the Lord is with thee; blessed art thou among women and blessed is the fruit of thy womb, Jesus. Holy Mary, Mother of God, pray for us sinners, now and at the hour of our death. Amen.

One *Hail Mary* is said on each of these three small beads.

The *Apostles' Creed* is said here (see page 18).

The *Gloria* is said on the big beads.
Glory be to the Father, and to the Son, and to the Holy Spirit; as it was in the beginning, is now and ever shall be, world without end. Amen.
This prayer is followed on each big bead with the *Our Father* prayer.

The *Gloria* is said on this small bead.

The *Our Father* prayer is said on this bead (see above).

Left: Christians in a church in Shanghai, in China, bow their heads in silent prayer. The photograph was taken in 1979, when the church was reopened for worship following years of official government opposition.

Saints and martyrs

Above: Saint Martin has been a popular saint for centuries, and hundreds of churches are named after him. This 17th century stained glass window shows the story for which he is best remembered.

Martin lived in the 4th century, and although he wanted to become a Christian, his parents insisted that he joined the Roman Army as a soldier. One bitter winter's day, as his legion rode through a city, Martin noticed a beggar who had only rags to wear, and who was desperate with cold and hunger. Filled with compassion, Martin drew his sword and cut his thick army cloak in half, giving one half to the beggar.

Martin later became a Christian and, refusing to fight any more, left the Roman Army and became a monk. Years later he was made Bishop of Tours, in France. Saint Martin's Day is celebrated on 11 November.

In the Middle Ages it could have seemed that the whole of Europe was on a march. Christians often went on pilgrimages (religious journeys) to pray at holy shrines. These were places where saints and martyrs were buried, or where important religious events had taken place. Praying at such shrines, it was thought, gave the pilgrims merit which they could not obtain in other ways. The journey showed God (and the saint) that the pilgrims had made a special effort for their sake. At the shrine pilgrims might ask for their sins to be forgiven, or to be cured of an illness.

Christians still make pilgrimages today, especially within the Roman Catholic and Orthodox churches. They still ask saints and martyrs to help them in their prayers to God. The cathedral of Vézelay, in France, was a famous shrine in the Middle Ages because it was thought to contain the bones of Mary Magdalene, a saint and friend of Jesus. Now Christians still visit Vézelay—not for the bones, which have been destroyed, but to share an experience of wonder at the building's great beauty, and to show the seriousness of their faith.

Saints

The Roman Catholic Church declares some very holy people to be saints after a long process called canonisation. The church considers each case very carefully, and all the evidence is studied in great detail.

Generally, two miracles have to be shown to have been performed through the saint's power. Some people are canonised centuries after their death, like Joan of Arc, the patron saint of France. She died in 1431 and was not canonised until 1920. Others are declared saints only a short time after their death, like Francis of Assisi, who died in 1226 and was canonised less than two years later.

Orthodox churches canonise saints as well, but the declaration of sainthood is not as formal. The Anglican Church has no formal process, but it too remembers holy people on particular days. In general, Protestant churches believe that people do not need to ask saints for help. But they recognise that many people called saints led holy lives, which are an example to all Christians.

Saint Francis

One person who receives universal admiration is Francis of Assisi. He is often remembered for his love of animals, but his life is remarkable for its simplicity and devotion to God. He captured the imagination of the Christian world through his deep faith, and seemed to mirror the way in which Jesus had lived. One writer said that, after Jesus lived, a wave of church leaders tried to follow him, pushing, shoving and arguing among themselves as they fought to put their feet in Jesus' footsteps. Far at the back of the crowd came the thin, shabbily-dressed figure of Saint Francis, quietly placing his feet exactly where his Lord had trodden.

Martyrs

A martyr is someone who is prepared to suffer, even to die, for their religious beliefs. Some saints are martyrs as well, but many martyrs are simply remembered for their courage under persecution. Most Christian churches have martyrs whose memory is honoured. The Friends often read stories which tell of their group's strong faith during persecution and hardship.

Modern figures of faith

Christians of all churches recognise the faith and devotion of many modern people, who show the sort of love and courage which they can admire and strive for themselves. They are examples, Christians believe, of what is possible with God's help.

Left: The statues of saints are often carried in processions. Many saints have their own days on which they are remembered, and which mark the day of their death (when they began a new life with God), not their birthdays.

These Peruvians are carrying three statues in procession to their village church. Saint Antony is at the front, Saint Bernard is next, and the last statue is of Jesus.

Left: Martin Luther King, a famous civil rights leader in the United States, was also a Baptist minister. He is shown here leading a protest march about the treatment of black people. The civil rights movement achieved much success through such non-violent protests, but Dr King was assassinated in 1968. Today many people recognise him as a martyr.

Far left: Archbishop Romero was called the 'voice of the voiceless' in El Salvador, because he spoke out against the government's treatment of poor people. In 1980 he was assassinated in San Salvador, while saying Mass in a chapel, by those who wanted to silence him.

The Virgin Mary

The Virgin Mary, Jesus' mother, is a beloved figure for millions of Christians. Shrines to her exist in many countries, especially around the Mediterranean and in South America. Thousands of churches throughout the world are named after her.

There is little about Mary in the Gospels. Only the Gospels of Matthew and Luke record the birth of Jesus, but these stress that Mary was an exceptional person—as she could be expected to be, if God chose her to give birth to his son. She is mentioned a few times in the Gospel stories of Jesus' teaching, and finally appears in the accounts of the crucifixion, standing at the foot of her son's cross.

Blessed among women

Mary is given a unique place by Roman Catholic and Orthodox Christians. She is regarded by them as a link between earth and heaven, and because she is Jesus' mother she has special access to him. She can, and does, it is thought, intercede with him on behalf of those who pray to her.

Mary was given the title of 'Mother of God' about 400 years after Jesus died, as a sign of her special role. Roman Catholic and some Orthodox traditions say that the birth of Jesus caused her no pain, and her body was not affected by it. Since the Holy Spirit, rather than a man, brought the seed of creation into Mary's womb she was still a virgin—and she remained a virgin all her life.

These churches also believe that Mary's body was taken into heaven when she died, in the same way as Jesus, and she is called the 'Queen of Heaven'. A feast day on 15 August celebrates that event.

Right: A mother and child in front of a statue of the Virgin Mary. The 'Queen of Heaven' wears a crown as a symbol of her heavenly role, but for many people she represents a simple love and understanding to which they can respond. She is asked to pray for them, as they pray for themselves and each other.

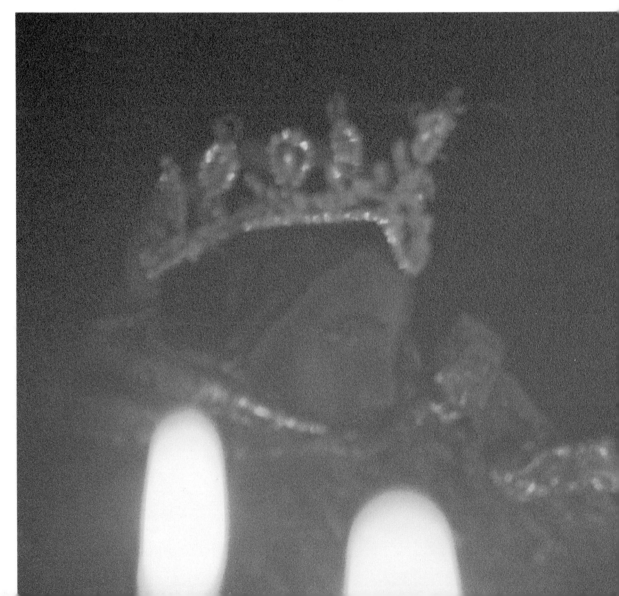

The Immaculate Conception

The Roman Catholic Church also says that Mary was born without sin. No ordinarily sinful person, they believe, could have given birth to the Son of God—and so Mary must have been free from sin all her life. This is called the Immaculate Conception, and means that Mary is unlike all other humans.

No other church shares this view of Mary. The Orthodox churches believe that Mary should be venerated (respected) more than any other human. But they also believe that Mary was human, not sinless.

Visions of Mary

Most people who pray to Mary simply hope for her help and guidance. But some have also experienced visions of Mary. They believe that they see Mary standing before them, even talking to them.

Religious people often report visions of holy figures, and there have been many accounts of this happening with Mary. Shrines have been established in several of these places—Lourdes in France, and Fatima in Portugal, are just two examples.

A controversial role

Most Protestant churches have felt uncomfortable about Mary's role. They believe people mistakenly worship her instead of Jesus. They do not agree with her place in prayer, and would not light candles and pray in front of statues or pictures of Mary—or of any other saint. Calvin believed that all prayer to Mary was against the Bible's message, although he agreed that God had given her high honour. These days, however, some Protestants and Catholics have begun to find common ground.

Religious communities

As Jesus was walking by the Sea of Galilee he saw two brothers, Simon, who was called Peter, and his brother Andrew, casting a net into the lake, for they were fishermen. Jesus said to them: "Follow me, and I will make you fishers of men." And they left their nets at once and followed him. Going on from there he saw another pair of brothers, James son of Zebedee and his brother John. He called them, and at once they left the boat and their father, and followed him.

This story from the Gospel of Matthew tells how the first Christianity community was formed. While most Christians have always led ordinary lives, some have felt the need to form special groups in which they can share their faith, and devote themselves more fully to Jesus.

Monasteries and convents

The first Christian monasteries were formed about 1,600 years ago, in Egypt. A monastery is a community of monks—men who have made vows of poverty, chastity (no sexual relations) and obedience. They live a simple life of prayer and work. Later, similar communities of women were also formed, with the same vows. Their communities are called convents, and their members, nuns.

In the western world Saint Benedict laid down a set of rules by which monasteries and convents were governed for centuries. He thought that monks and nuns should always be busy—with prayer, work and reading holy books.

Other organisations

The Benedictine ideas spread, and soon other Christian groups were formed. Many still gave much of their time to worship, offering praise to God and prayers for the world. Others were involved in caring for the poor, the sick and the dying, and in other kinds of service. The Dominicans became famous for their teaching and learning; the Jesuits for their stress on the importance of education. Saint Teresa of Avila formed an order of nuns called the Carmelites, and Saint Clare's 'Poor Clare' nuns owned nothing, relying on God's mercy to provide them with food and shelter.

Modern communities

Some of today's groups are like the Iona Community, which has its headquarters on the Scottish island of Iona. The people who belong to it are not monks or nuns, but ordinary people with families and jobs, who share a life of prayer, social concern and commitment to God. They work for the poor, run camps for young people, and give time, prayer and money to their community fund. Some of their members live in Scotland, while others work as far away as Africa and Asia.

There are still many Orthodox, Roman Catholic and Anglican communities. But a few offer membership to all Christians, rather than only to their own group. Taizé, in France, is one example. Roger Schütz, a Swiss Protestant, believed that Christians needed a place to work together, towards love and care for all. He began the Taizé community after World War II, and it now has both Roman Catholic as well as Protestant members. Thousands of people have shared the experience it offers—a reconciling of differences, and a common love and peace with God.

Below: Anglican nuns take a group of children from the Nazareth kindergarten in Tokyo, to be blessed by the local bishop. Many religious communities are active in education and child care.

Left: A nun on pilgrimage in Poland stops to read from her office book; part of her daily round of worship. The offices, or set forms of prayer, are traditionally said seven times each day. Mattins, the first office of the day, is said at about 2am; Compline, the last, is said at about 8pm. Today, however, many nuns and monks say only four offices each day.

Left: Brother Roger Schütz, founder of the Taizé community, speaks in their crowded church during a Sunday service. His words are immediately translated into different languages, for thousands of people from all over the world visit Taizé to pray with the Brothers. One Pope described Taizé as ''that little springtime'' of the Christian church.

Joining the church

Jesus came from Nazareth in Galilee and was baptised in the Jordan by John. No sooner had he come up out of the water than he saw the heavens torn apart and the Spirit, like a dove, descending on him. And a voice came from heaven: "You are my Son, my Beloved, my favour rests on you."

This account of Jesus' baptism by John the Baptist is from the Gospel of Mark. The event forms the basis for the baptism ceremonies used in nearly all Christian churches when new members are admitted. The word 'baptism' means 'immersion', and that is why some churches demand that new members should be completely immersed in water. Because Jesus was baptised in a river —in 'living water'—some also hold their ceremonies in a nearby river or lake.

The meaning of baptism
Most Christians regard baptism as an outward, physical sign of re-birth. It marks the start of a new life which they share with other Christians, and the water is a symbol of the way in which sin was removed from human life by Jesus.

Different interpretations
Not all Christians believe exactly the same things about baptism, and so not all groups perform them in the same way. The Baptist churches baptise only believers, since they hold that infants cannot make a personal commitment to Christ. Their baptism statements relate the ceremony to a future world of experience: "as the body is buried under water and rises again, so shall the bodies of the faithful be raised by the power of Christ." Many Baptist churches have a pool built under the main floor, which is used for total immersion.

Many Pentecostal churches also practise believers' baptism. Sometimes whole groups are baptised together, with each person making a personal statement of their belief in Jesus as the living God, or in him as saviour.

The Society of Friends believes only in a spiritual baptism. So they do not use a ceremony at all, for they believe that it is unnecessary to display an outward sign—the washing in water—as a symbol of an inward state. For similar reasons, the Salvation Army does not practise baptism.

Child baptism
The Roman Catholic, Orthodox and most Protestant churches baptise children when they are still babies. Russian Orthodox babies are traditionally baptised when they are 8 days old; the same day of life on which the baby Jesus would have been circumcised as a Jew. All Orthodox babies are baptised by total immersion in the holy water of the font, a large basin in the church. Roman Catholic, Anglican and Protestant babies are baptised by being sprinkled with holy or blessed water from the font.

As the water touches the baby, the priest or minister makes a statement about Christian belief, and traces the sign of the cross on the baby's forehead. God-parents (other adults chosen by the baby's parents) promise to help the child understand Christian belief as he or she grows up.

Left: The baptism of a child is a family occasion in two ways: the child's family is celebrating the birth of a new member, and the church is welcoming the baby into its own family.

This Greek Orthodox baby has been dipped in water three times—for belief in the Trinity, for the death of past sins, and for a new life in Jesus.

Left: A river baptism in the Congo. The ministers are standing at the back, and the newly-baptised have just emerged from the river's 'living' water.

Almost certainly, the words used at this ceremony will be those used throughout the Christian world: ''I baptise you in the name of the Father, and of the Son, and of the Holy Spirit''.

Do this in memory...

The Bible has several records of the meal which Jesus shared with his companions on the night of his arrest. As he broke bread and passed it to his friends, Jesus said: "This is my body which is given for you; do this in memory of me." Then, as he passed the wine, he said: "This is the new covenant made in my blood. Whenever you drink it, do this in memory of me."

This meal is called the Last Supper. For most Christians it is the basis for their central ceremony.

The Communion service

A variety of names is used to describe the ceremony. 'Communion' means 'sharing'; another common name is 'Eucharist' which is the Greek word for 'thanksgiving'. In this way Christians share in the memory of Jesus' death and resurrection, and they thank God for the gift of his son.

Roman Catholics call their service the Mass, a word that probably comes from the Latin phrase which priests used at the end: 'ite missa est', or 'go, you are dismissed'. The Orthodox 'Divine Liturgy' means 'holy service', and the word 'service' shows that people are serving God in the ceremony.

Some Protestant churches simply use the name 'Lord's Supper', or the 'Breaking of Bread'. The first term refers to the Last Supper, and the second is taken from the Bible, where early Christians are recorded 'breaking bread' as they prayed together.

Methods of celebrating

Roman Catholic churches celebrate Mass each day, and so do some Anglican churches. Others celebrate only on Sundays and other feast days. United Reformed and Baptist churches hold their service less frequently; perhaps once a month.

Most Roman Catholics receive only a wafer of bread, and no wine. The Orthodox receive a small piece of bread dipped in wine from a long spoon. In some Protestant churches each person receives a small glass of wine, but in others they sip from the same cup, in turn.

Different beliefs

Many churches believe the Last Supper was the Jewish Passover meal. They use flat wafers of bread, because no yeast would have been put into bread during Passover. Orthodox churches, however, use risen bread because they do not believe the Last Supper was a Passover meal at all.

Orthodox and Catholic worshippers believe that the bread and wine become the body and blood of Jesus, during the prayer when these are offered to God and consecrated (made holy). The bread and wine still *look* the same, but the miracle of Jesus' resurrection makes them a real part of him. So he is physically present, and worshippers are able to experience him, and to share in his sacrifice.

Most Protestants do not believe that such a change takes place. Many of their churches use ordinary bread instead of the special wafers, because they believe the Last Supper cannot be exactly duplicated. Some also prefer to use non-alcoholic wine.

Protestant tradition is also reflected in those churches where the bread and wine are passed around by members of the congregation, rather than by their ministers. All these things show their understanding of the ceremony's meaning—to share their food and drink as Jesus commanded, in faith, hope and remembrance of him.

Below: Children in the Orthodox churches share in the Divine Liturgy from baptism. All Orthodox worshippers receive the bread, dipped in the wine, from a spoon. A deacon (server) holds a cloth under the spoon so that nothing is spilt on the floor.

Left: A Roman Catholic priest holds up the wafer of bread and the chalice (cup) of wine for adoration. This reflects the Catholic belief that the bread and wine have become the body and blood of Jesus Christ.

Below: A Protestant outdoor Communion. When there are a lot of people at a service several ministers distribute the bread and wine. You can see the chalices being offered—the bread has already been shared.

Living in the church

Right: A Christian summer holiday camp in the United States. These children are being taught how to join in the services of their church. The way in which the minister performs his role is explained, so that the children's experiences will be more interesting. Some of them may help the minister during church services when they are older, like the teenagers in this photograph.

Many Christian families expect their children to grow up within their own church, and if their children have been baptised, they are already church members. Roman Catholic children generally attend church schools, and most other groups provide religious training for their children. Many include this within services, or hold week-day evening, or Sunday morning, classes.

A personal experience

The Christian Brethren also expect the children within their group to be converted. "Conversion", they say, "does not depend on being brought up a Christian or living in a Christian country; being a church member or being religious. It is something personal, and as life-long as getting married. It is between each individual and Jesus Christ."

This desire for personal experience is shared by all Christians, but it is approached in different ways. A small boy dressed in his best clothes and carrying a candle, who enters his church on the first Sunday after Easter, may not have experienced conversion in the Brethren sense. But he is to receive his First Communion, an important stage in growing up within the Roman Catholic Church.

Confirmation

Full membership of the Orthodox churches takes place when children are very young. The ceremony occurs straight after baptism, when a priest applies holy ointment to many parts of the baby's body, in the sign of a cross. Children participate in the Divine Liturgy from that time.

Most other churches accept children as full members when they are teenagers. The Confirmation services in the Roman Catholic and Anglican churches are performed by a local bishop, who puts his hands on the head of each person who kneels before him. All of them promise to be faithful for the rest of their lives. Most Anglicans receive their First Communion directly after their Confirmation, but Roman Catholics have usually shared in that already.

Methodists and most other Protestants hold a ceremony in which young people make their faithful promises, and are admitted into the full responsibilities and privileges of church membership.

Marriage

Christians believe that marriage is central to human life, because it marks the beginning of a new family and a new generation. All churches encourage their members to hold weddings in God's sight, and under his blessing. Many traditions have developed to symbolise the value of this commitment made between men and women.

Christians also believe, as the Bible says, that marriage can only be with a single partner, and is made for life. Divorce and remarriage have often caused difficulties, and some groups do not recognise divorce at all. Any of their members who have obtained a civil divorce cannot remarry in church.

Death

Christians are taught that Jesus will return to the world to rule forever, and on that day the dead will rise to join in his glory. In the past most believed that they should be buried, not cremated, so that their earthly bodies could rise on Judgement Day. Today, however, many do not interpret this in such literal terms, and do not mind whether they are buried or cremated.

Left: A wedding in a Syrian Orthodox church. During an Orthodox wedding service the couple exchange rings, and sip wine three times from the same cup. The priest then leads them in a procession three times around the church, while hymns and prayers are sung. Promises are made on their behalf, and they wear crowns to symbolise their importance to each other.

Left: On All Souls' Day many Christians remember those who have died, and this Mexican woman and child are arranging flowers on a grave. The coloured cross and streamers suggest life rather than death—for Christians are taught that death is just the beginning of a new life with God.

Easter

Easter is the most important Christian festival. It is the time when their central belief—the death and resurrection of Jesus Christ—is celebrated. After the tragedy of Good Friday, when Jesus' death on the cross is remembered, the Christian world bursts with joy on Easter Day, the following Sunday, which marks his resurrection. Their delight and exhilaration are all the greater because of what precedes Easter: Lent, a period of discipline and self-denial.

Lent

The season of Lent lasts for forty days. Its name comes from an old word for 'spring'—because Easter is a springtime festival in the northern hemisphere. Lent was originally used to prepare prospective Christians for baptism, but today it is spent by many in remembering Jesus' time in the wilderness, as a preparation for Easter.

Ash Wednesday is the first day of Lent, and in some parts of the church Christians receive a spot of ash on their foreheads, as a sign of their sorrow for their sins, and as a reminder of death.

Lent is sometimes called the Great Fast in Orthodox churches, and many Christians fast (do without certain foods) at this time. Some do not eat meat; others avoid fats, or wine, or sweet things. Not all Christians mark Lent, but some deliberately do without something they normally enjoy. They believe this helps them to understand the suffering which Jesus experienced. Some churches even stop using cheerful tunes and hymns during Lent, and play only solemn music.

Palm Sunday

This day is the first in Holy Week, the week before Easter. It marks the day when Jesus rode into Jerusalem on a donkey, and was welcomed by crowds who threw down palm branches to greet him. This is re-told around the world in Palm Sunday processions and plays. Some Christians carry enormous palm branches, while others use small crosses made from palm leaves which have been blessed by a priest. The palm crosses link Palm Sunday with Good Friday, and are also burned the following year to make the ash used during Ash Wednesday services.

Far left: Many Christians parade through the streets during Holy Week, showing public repentance for their sins. This Mexican penitent is dressed completely in black as a sign of sorrow. The cross with the figure of Jesus on it which she is holding is called a crucifix.

Left: A group of Christians in Guatemala carry a statue of Jesus into their village church on Easter Day. The vivid colours of the decorations reflect the day's happiness. Gifts of money for the church's work have been pinned to the statue's robes, and you can see the head of a smaller statue peeping through the robes—a local saint is sharing in the celebrations!

Holy Week

Processions and plays continue during Holy Week. Some processions are especially famous, like those in Seville, in Spain. Penitents dressed completely in black, with even their faces masked from view, parade to show their sorrow for their sins. Many carry crosses, and statues of Jesus, through the streets of their town.

Passion plays are also performed during Holy Week. In this case 'passion' means suffering, and the plays are based on the Gospel stories about Jesus' arrest and trial, and his death on the cross.

As Easter weekend approaches many churches take down decorations, and cover those which they cannot remove. They are preparing to mourn Jesus' death.

The Thursday before Easter is called Maundy Thursday. It commemorates the Last Supper, and the washing of his companions' feet by Jesus. Many church leaders re-enact the foot-washing, and even the Pope, archbishops and patriarchs kneel down before ordinary people to perform this. It reminds everyone of Jesus' command that his followers should serve others.

Good Friday

Good Friday is called 'Good', perhaps because on that day Jesus displayed the greatest sort of goodness possible. It is the most solemn day in the Christian year. Church services take place, often from noon until 3 pm, the hours thought to represent Jesus' time on the cross. Some Christians spend the whole day in prayer and silent meditation.

Easter Day

Most Christians hold services which celebrate the beginning of Easter Day, at midnight on Easter Saturday. Many use candlelight as a sign that Christ has risen from death—and those words are used in their greetings to each other. "Christ has risen!" cries the priest. "He has risen indeed!" replies the congregation. Prayers of praise and thanksgiving, sermons of joy and hymns of triumph ring out around the Christian world. The truth of the resurrection is, for Christians, a living reality.

Forty days later comes the festival of Ascension Day, when Christ is believed to have been taken into heaven by God.

Christmas

Far right: Jesus is often referred to as the 'lamb of God'; a sign of the sacrifice God made through him, for lambs were offered in sacrifice in the ancient Jewish Temple.

The lamb this monk is carrying into a Christmas service will also remind people of the shepherds' visit to the stable.

Below: A Christmas Eve crowd outside the Church of the Nativity, in Bethlehem. Some Christians believe the church stands on the exact spot where Jesus was born.

Christmas is the second great festival of the Christian year, and celebrates the birth of Jesus. It begins four Sundays before Christmas Day with the season of Advent, a time of expectation and preparation.

The word 'Christmas' comes from the Old English 'Chrestes Maesses', or 'Christ's Mass'. All except some Orthodox churches celebrate it on 25 December. (The difference is caused by changes to the calendar with which those churches do not agree: they still use 7 January.) The December date was originally chosen by the Emperor Constantine to coincide with a Roman sun festival; no-one knows the exact day when Jesus was born. Choosing that date was a way of turning an existing celebration into a Christian one. In the northern hemisphere, where it falls in the middle of winter, Christmas is seen as a promise of the new life which Jesus brings.

Christians gather in churches all over the world late on Christmas Eve, the day before Christmas. They hold midnight services, sing carols and hymns, and offer thanks for the birth of Jesus. Crib scenes are often set up in churches, with models of Jesus, Mary and Joseph in the stable at Bethlehem where Jesus is thought to have been born. The shepherds whom the Bible says were the first to visit the baby Jesus, and the Magi (wise men) who arrived later to pay him homage as the new king, often appear around the crib as well.

Epiphany

Twelve days after Christmas comes Epiphany; a Greek word which means 'showing forth'. This marks Jesus' baptism in the river Jordan. The showing of Jesus to the Magi, people from outside the Jewish world, is also remembered.

Celebrations

Every Sunday is a feast day for Christians, because it marks the rising of Jesus from the dead. In addition, as well as Easter and Christmas, there are many other occasions in the year for prayer and rejoicing.

All Saints' Day

All Saints' Day is in memory of every saint, including those who are unknown to the world and do not have a special day of their own. This festival often takes on a local flavour, and traditional customs are mixed with Christian prayer and song. In Guatemala, horses are raced through the streets of Todos Santos, and a seven metre kite is launched from a cemetery in Santiago de Sacatepequez. The kite symbolises the release of souls from their earthly bodies, for their journey to join God in heaven.

Thanksgiving

Harvest festivals occur all over the world, and are used by Christians to thank God for the food provided by the earth and sea. Many people bring samples of their crops into church to be blessed, and church leaders often parade to fields and fishing harbours to hold services there.

Thanksgiving for being saved from plague, famine and other disasters is also common. In Venice, for example, a bridge of boats is built on the third Sunday in July each year. The bridge stretches between the main island and another, where the Church of the Redentore (the Redeemer) was built in the 16th century as a thanks offering for the end of a plague. The sky is bright with fireworks and the city resounds with music as Venice thanks God for its deliverance.

The Church of the Nazarites in Africa has several great festivals in memory of their leader, Isaiah Shembe. Each year, in January and July, they gather at a mountain where Shembe experienced visions of Jesus. The people feast, dance, and sing their thanks for God's help.

Some churches believe that only those festivals mentioned in the Bible should be celebrated by their members. They think that links with other traditions make festivals un-Christian. Most Christians, however, enjoy responding to God in such a variety of ways.

Below: The Festival of the Trays is celebrated in the town of Tomar, in Portugal, every four years. It is probably linked to an ancient harvest festival held in Roman times. Each tray contains 30 bread rolls which are decorated with flowers and streamers, and crowned with a flower cross. The trays are carried through the streets of Tomar to the main church, where they are blessed. Then the rolls, together with meat and wine, are given to the town's poor.

Below: On Saint Lucia Day in Sweden young girls parade in white dresses, with crowns of flowers and candles in their hair. This procession is part of a Lutheran church service in the city of Malmö.

Very little is known about Saint Lucia, but her day (13 December) has become one of national importance in Sweden.

Below: A gypsy pilgrimage to the seaside town of Saintes-Maries-de-la-Mer in France, where the memory of Mary Magdalene and Mary of Bethany is celebrated. The gypsies are carrying their own statue of the Virgin Mary into the water, where they will ask for her blessing on their lives, during the coming year.

Which church?

Missionaries

During the past few hundred years western Christians sent missionaries to Africa, India and the far East. They believed that everyone should be told about Jesus, but the differences so apparent between Christian groups often led to confusion and bewilderment. The various missionaries were seldom sympathetic to each other's views, and their basic beliefs often seemed to conflict. They prayed in different languages and in different ways—and the tunes and rhythms of their hymns were completely foreign to the new countries' cultures. Some missionaries, too, lacked understanding or respect for the people of the lands they visited.

The legacy of such problems has not yet been completely solved, but many Christian churches in Africa and Asia have grown strong roots of their own, developing ways to interpret belief which make the best sense to them. Some, in turn, have sent their own missions to western countries and so shared their understandings with others.

The ecumenical movement

The Greek word 'ecumenical' means 'the whole world', and it is used to describe ways in which Christian groups might resolve their differences. The Church of South India provided one solution to the confusion and bitterness of the past. Formed in 1947, it brought together the Anglican, Methodist, Presbyterian and Congregational churches of southern India. Now all worship together, and share a common belief.

One year later the World Council of Churches was formed. Its headquarters are in Geneva, in Switzerland, and it has member churches in many countries. More than 300 different Christian groups belong to the Council, including Orthodox, Anglican, Methodist, Baptist, Pentecostal and United Reformed churches. The Roman Catholic Church is not a full member, but it has sent observers since 1968.

Not all churches believe that the ecumenical movement is right. They may disagree with other groups on minor issues, or on more important ones. If the issues seem very important it is difficult for the churches to see value in discussion. Those who believe that their interpretation of Jesus is the only possible truth may be

unable to find ways to work in harmony with groups who hold opposing views.

Today—and tomorrow

Christians who regard Jesus as the focus of their religious belief must decide if they want to join a church—and if so, which one. Today there is a growing feeling among some that Christians need not necessarily attend church, or any other religious meeting. They may believe their individual faith can best be expressed in less formal ways. Others find an intimate sense of community in Jesus through small, private groups. While most church leaders reject these ideas, many would agree that churches sometimes fail to provide ways for their members to experience such closeness.

The 20th century has seen changes in Christian attitudes. Many groups are more tolerant of other forms of Christian belief, as well as of other religions. Church leaders are seen to show respect for one another, and to make time to meet and talk. But the belief stated in an old hymn, "one Church, one Faith, one Lord", seems still to be reserved for a distant future.

Far left: A Communion service in the Church of South India. The traditions of the founding churches in this group have been combined, so that all can share equally in the worship. The priest on the left is preparing to pass around separate glasses of wine for each member of the group—a common custom amongst Presbyterians and Methodists.

Left: The traditions of Christian worship used by the Yoruba in Africa have been adapted by some South American churches. Here, Brazilian Christians kneel down before a statue of Jesus, whose outstretched arms seem to replace the symbol of the cross.

Left: The World Council of Churches holds services in which all their member churches can participate. Here you can see leaders from many Orthodox and Protestant groups sharing common worship at a conference.

Responding in faith

Jesus explained his healings and teachings in terms of the future kingdom of God, when God's rule would be shared by people. Meanwhile, his message was also concerned with the way people responded to their present human life. He demanded that his followers should show care and love for others, in response to his own love for them. Talking of the hungry, the homeless and the sick, Jesus said: "I tell you this. Anything you do for one of those, however humble, you do for me." So Christians believe they must respond to what God intends for the whole world, through their ordinary actions.

This challenge is hard to resolve, and it has had hundreds of different expressions. Many Christians try to combine prayer with practical actions. This has often led them into conflict with governments and other authorities, as well as their own churches.

Government opposition

In the twentieth century Christians in the Soviet Union and eastern Europe had to deal with Communist governments that promoted atheism. In Albania all expression of religious belief was made illegal and most other Communist governments discouraged it. In such situations Christians must find a way to balance the demands of their religious beliefs with the demands of their government.

In some Communist countries Christianity flourished despite the efforts of governments. The Roman Catholic Church in Poland, for example, had an extremely large and loyal following. When Communist rule began to collapse in the late 1980s, the Orthodox churches gained new strength.

It was not only in Communist countries that Christians faced difficulties. The white people who governed South Africa until 1994 saw themselves as leading a 'Christian nation' but they supported a system called apartheid. Under apartheid, white people were given preferential treatment over black people. Desmond Tutu, an Anglican leader in South Africa, argued that Christians cannot accept a system which values people differently, according to the colour of their skin. The government tried to silence Tutu by threatening him and withdrawing his passport but he continued his protests.

What difference does it make?

These statements come from Christians of many different groups, who are trying to express faith through their ordinary lives.

It's very hard to love everyone, but you should never hate anyone for what they do. Hate just gives the devil a free hand.

I don't think faith ever stops you, or hinders you doing what you want. It's not like a full stop—it's a dash that helps you carry on.

Jesus told us we shouldn't store up treasures on earth. It's hard to work out how to respond to that, and even harder to carry it out. I'm trying to decide if I should give away the thing I most value; I think I care too much about it. Doing that would help free me, to concentrate on God. But I don't know if I can bear to!

When my parents died I couldn't believe in Christ any more. Later I was able to believe again, but in a different way. Now I think my original faith was wrong—God doesn't exist to hand out presents, and he can't protect us from the reality of death.

I think my faith has to carry over from Sunday to Monday. I don't accept orders from alcoholic drink manufacturers for my cardboard box factory, because I believe alcohol is dangerous and wrong. People should use their bodies for the glory of God, not destroy them with drink.

I try to give my faults to God, in prayer. Some problems—like selfishness—occur a lot, and I have to ask for his help time and again.

Third World aid

Many Christians work with the poor and oppressed in their own countries, or in other parts of the world. Organisations such as Christian Aid believe that the best way to solve the world's inequalities is to share its resources more fairly. So they help Third World countries fight disease and hunger by providing money, materials and machinery, and by sharing knowledge with local people.

Revolution

Camilo Torres, a Roman Catholic priest in Colombia, spoke for many when he argued that only revolution could permanently improve life for the poor. "It is the only effective and large-scale way of carrying out works of love for everyone," he said.

Torres had to leave the church because of his involvement with South American guerilla movements, and he was killed in fighting a few years later. But the ideas have not died with him. Today, Jesuit priests form part of the revolutionary government in Nicaragua, and Christians still passionately argue the rights and wrongs of political ideas and political involvement.

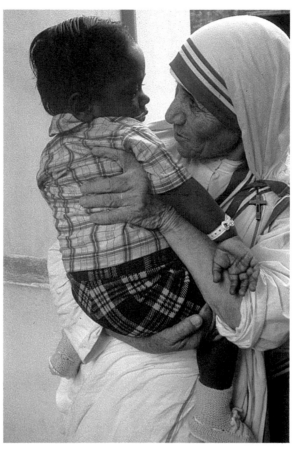

Left: "Money is not enough. Don't just give me money, or things I can get for the asking. My people need you to love them." These words from Mother Teresa, a Roman Catholic nun, sum up her work among the poor and homeless of Calcutta. She devoted her life to caring for the sick and dying in India, and founded an order of nuns which carries out such work in other countries as well.

Mother Teresa, who died in 1997, did not try to change the way in which countries are governed. Her only concern was to help people who had no one else to care for them.

Far left: Archbishop Desmond Tutu speaks to a crowd in Johannesburg. His fight against apartheid was based on his understanding of the Christian faith. Since apartheid came to an end he has worked to develop good relations between the black and white peoples of South Africa.

Left: This South American poster shows Jesus as a guerilla fighter. Many revolutionary groups use the Gospel's message in their struggle to bring freedom and equality to the world.

Further information

A glossary of useful words

angel a heavenly being. The word means 'messenger', and angels often appear in the Bible as God's messengers and attendants.

Apocrypha a collection of 13 books included in the Roman Catholic Bible, but not usually accepted by other churches as holy scripture. The word means 'hidden things'.

apostles the title given to some of the people who spread the news of Jesus' life and teaching. It is usually reserved for the first 12 disciples, together with Saint Paul and Saint Matthias.

circumcision the removal of the foreskin from the penis in males.

Communion a sharing. The act of receiving bread and wine during the Eucharist, the central Christian service. The term 'Communion', or 'Holy Communion', is also used for the Eucharist service itself.

congregation the people who have gathered together for worship.

consecration making holy.

conversion a 'turn about'. The acceptance of Jesus as saviour and God.

Creed a statement of belief. There are two main Creeds used by Christians; the Apostles' Creed, and the Nicene Creed. The Apostles' Creed was first referred to in AD 390, but it probably has an even earlier history. Its name comes from an old belief that it was written by the apostles. It is not used by the Orthodox Churches. The Nicene Creed was written by the Council of Nicaea in AD 325, but the versions used now were agreed at the Council of Constantinople in AD 381. Then, in the 9th century, a phrase was added to the Nicene Creed about the Holy Spirit. This has never been accepted by the Orthodox Churches, so two versions exist today.

cremation the burning of bodies after death, instead of burying them.

crucifix a model of Jesus on the cross.

devil an evil spirit. When the word has a capital D it refers to the chief spirit of evil, the enemy of God and people, often called Satan.

divine sharing the nature and power of God.

disciples the title given to Jesus' original 12 companions, and to anyone who follows him now.

eternal everlasting.

Eucharist thanksgiving. One of the names for the central Christian service, often called the Mass, or Holy Communion, or the Lord's Supper.

font a large basin for holding the water used in baptism.

halo a circle of light, often used in paintings around the heads of Jesus and the saints.

heaven the eternal kingdom where God, the saints, and the angels are, and where Christians hope to be after death.

hell the traditional place of punishment for sinners after death; the exclusion from God's presence.

incarnation to become flesh. The belief that God the Son became a human being, Jesus.

liturgy public worship. The order of service in a church.

parable a story with a hidden meaning. Jesus' teaching often used parables.

parish the district which 'belongs' to a church.

pater noster the Latin words for 'Our Father'. It refers to the Lord's Prayer, which begins with those words.

penitent someone who shows they are sorry for their sins.

Reformation the reform movement in the Roman Catholic Church which led to the formation of the Protestant Churches.

repentance sorrow for sins, and the determination to try to do better.

resurrection raised up. The raising of Jesus from death by God, and the belief that all people will rise from death on Judgement Day.

sacrament a visible sign of God's power.

sanctuary the part of a church which contains the altar. It is the most important and sacred part of the building.

scripture the Christian Bible.

soul the eternal part of human life, separate from the physical part. Some Christians believe that souls are freed from their bodies after death, to join God in heaven.

synagogue a meeting house for Jewish worship.

temple a holy building.

Trinity the belief that the One God exists in three persons; God the Father, God the Son, and God the Holy Spirit.

veneration to treat something with deep respect and reverence.

The Christian calendar

Christians use the birth of Jesus as the central point in history. The exact date of this is unknown, but the calculations of a monk in the 6th century were used for hundreds of years. In his system Jesus' birth divided history into BC and AD: history before and after that day. AD stands for 'Anno Domini', the Latin words for 'in the year of our Lord'. It refers to the period since the birth of Jesus. BC stands for 'Before Christ', and refers to the period before Jesus was born.

The Gospels say that Jesus was born during the reign of King Herod the Great. Historians now know, however, that Herod died in 4 BC, and so it is quite possible that Jesus was really born two or three years before Herod died: perhaps in 6 or 7 BC, rather than in AD 1.

Different calendars

Julius Caesar's calendar (called the Julian calendar) was used in the Christian world until the 16th century. Then, in 1582, Pope Gregory XIII introduced a new calendar—called the Gregorian calendar after him. The Julian calendar had not properly fitted the Earth's movements around the Sun, and so it was not accurate.

The Gregorian system was adopted by most churches, and almost every country in the world has based its civil calendar on the Gregorian one. Some Orthodox churches still prefer to use the Julian calendar, and that is why their Christmas and Easter celebrations happen at different times from the rest of the Christian world. (The difference is usually about 13 days.) However, many Greek Orthodox, and most Orthodox churches in the United States, use the Gregorian calendar.

Fixed and moveable dates

The Christian year begins with Advent, four Sundays before Christmas. Some festivals are celebrated on fixed days, and so they happen at the same time each year: Christmas is one of these. Other festival dates (like Easter) are worked out from the moon's movements, which do not match the ordinary civil calendar. So those festivals are celebrated at slightly different times from year to year.

Major dates	
January 6	Epiphany
January 7	Christmas in some Orthodox Churches
January 19	Epiphany★
February 2	Candlemass
February 14	Hypapante★ *The presentation of the infant Jesus in the Temple*
February/March	Ash Wednesday *The first day of Lent* (Western)
March/April	Palm Sunday Holy Week Easter
March 25	Annunciation of the Blessed Virgin Mary
April 7	Annunciation of the Mother of God (Virgin Mary)★
April/May	Orthodox Sunday★ *The first day of Lent* (Orthodox) The Great Fast★ Easter, or the Feast of Feasts★
May/June	Pentecost/Whitsun Trinity Sunday Corpus Christi Feast of All Saints★
August	Falling Asleep of the Mother of God★ Assumption of the Blessed Virgin Mary
September 21	Nativity of the Mother of God★
September 27	Exaltation of the Holy Cross★
November 1	All Saints' Day
November/ December	Advent Sunday
December 4	Presentation of the Mother of God in the Temple★
December 8	Immaculate Conception of the Blessed Virgin Mary
December 25	Christmas

★ shows the Orthodox dates for their major festivals. The other entries are celebrated by many Christian groups, although some are kept only by Roman Catholics.

Books for further reading

Books for younger readers
The Story of Christianity Michael Collins and Matthew Price (Dorling Kindersley, 1999)
Christianity for Today Carrie Mercier (Oxford University Press, 1997)
Christianity Sue Penney (Heinemann Library, 2000)
I Am a Roman Catholic B. Pettenuzzo (Watts Books, 2001)
What Do We Know About Christianity? Carol Watson (Hodder Wayland, 1997)

Books for older readers/teachers
A Real Christian: The Life of John Wesley Kenneth J. Collins (Abingdon Press, 1999)
Why Angels Fall: A Journey Through Orthodox Europe from Byzantium to Kosovo Victoria Clarke (St Martins Press, 2000)
Methodism and the Future of Christianity Jane Craske and Clive Marsh (Continuum Publishing Group, 2000)
Two Thousand Years Nicola Currie (Lion Publishing, 1999)
Baptist Church Margaret Griffin and Paul Bellingham (Staffordshire Education, 1997)
The Oxford Companion to Christian Thought ed. Adrian Hastings (Oxford University Press, 2000)
New Catholics for a New Century Arthur Jones (Thomas More Press, 2000)
Mere Christianity C.S. Lewis (Fount, 1997)
The Good Enough Catholic: A Guide for the Perplexed Paul Wilkes (Ballantyne Books, 1997)

Websites

http://www.catholic.org/
A starting point for information about the Roman Catholic Church

http://www.churches.com
http://www.rhall.org.uk/methodist
http://www.unitarian.org.uk
These websites provide information about Methodism and other Protestant Non-Conformist Churches

Places to visit

There are so many buildings of Christian importance and interest in Britain that it is impossible to list them all here. Monasteries, convents, abbeys, cathedrals, churches, chapels, missions and meeting houses – all exist, and many of them can be visited. Cathedrals and abbeys will always be open during daylight hours, and so will most churches – although some churches are now locked when they are not is use.

Particular places of local interest near to you can generally be found: you may know of one in your area, or you can ask your library for suggestions. Tourist offices will also be able to help. Many other places can be found in the Yellow Pages of the telephone directory (look under 'Religious organisations', or 'Churches'). Church groups welcome visitors to their buildings, and you can watch (or join in) their services if you want to. If you only want to look at the buildings make sure you know when services are held, so that you do not interrupt them. Most places provide guidebooks, leaflets or notes to make you visit more interesting.

Helpful organisations

These organisations are some of many that offer help and information. Don't forget to enclose a stamped addressed envelope when you write.

The British Council of Churches
35 - 41 Lower Marsh, London SE1 7RL

Catholic Education Service
39 Eccleston Square, London SW1V

Christian Education Movement
Royal Buildings Victoria Street, Derby DE1 1GW

Church of England Information Office
Church House, Great Smith Street
London SW1P 3NZ

The Religious Society of Friends (Quakers)
Friends House, Euston Road
London NW1 2BJ

The Free Church Federal Council
27 Tavistock Square, London WC1H 9HH

Index

Numbers in heavy type refer to picture captions, or to the pictures themselves.